HANDS-OFF MANAGEMENT
THE ENTREPRENEUR'S GUIDE TO SELF-RUNNING BUSINESSES

How to step away from daily operations and build winning teams

CLAUDIO PINHO JUNIOR

Claudio Pinho Junior

HANDS-OFF MANAGEMENT:
THE ENTREPRENEUR'S GUIDE TO SELF-RUNNING BUSINESS
Editorial Coordination:
Gilson Mello

Graphic Design:
Flórida Business Academy

Proofreading, Editing, and Copyediting:
Fabiana Mello

General Direction:
Gilson Mello

All rights reserved and protected under Law No. 9.610, of 02/19/1998.

The total or partial reproduction of this book by any means (electronic, mechanical, photographic, recording, and others) without prior written authorization from the publisher is strictly prohibited.

First Edition 2024

International Cataloging Data in Publication (CIP)
Pinho Junior, Claudio
Hands-off management:
The entrepreneur's guide to self-running business
Claudio Pinho Junior; Orlando-FL: Flórida Business Academy
Business, 2024.
141 p.
ISBN: 9798342899031
1. Business 2. Personal fulfillment. 3 Success

Contents

Preface -- 5

Introduction -- 9

Chapter 1:

Architecting Your Self-Managed Business -------------------- 15

Chapter 2:

The Power of Efficient Processes -------------------------------- 25

Chapter 3:

The Art of Effective Delegation ---------------------------------- 33

Chapter 4:

Automating for Success --- 43

Chapter 5:

Measuring Success: The KPIs That Matter -------------------- 53

Chapter 6:

Leading from a Distance ---63

Chapter 7:

Cultivating Autonomy in the Team ----------------------------- 73

Chapter 8:

Building a Championship Team ---------------------------------- 83

Chapter 9:

Mastering Time for Leaders --- 93

Chapter 10:

Agility in Business -- 103

Chapter 11:

Communication That Transforms -------------------------------- 113

Chapter 12:

The Future is Now: Staying Ahead ------------------------------ 123

Conclusion -- 133

Claudio Pinho Junior

When I embarked on my journey into entrepreneurship, I had big dreams and aspirations, but I also faced a number of challenges that, at first glance, seemed insurmountable. Over the course of more than 28 years in the business world, I have had the opportunity to learn from every success and, most importantly, from every mistake. Running businesses in Brazil and the United States, across different sectors, has taught me that the key to a thriving and sustainable company is its ability to operate independently, with an engaged team and well-defined processes.

This book, "Hands-off management: The entrepreneur's guide to self-running business", is born from my own experience in building companies that extend beyond me as the founder. From establishing businesses such as Cenetram Centro de Educação de Trânsito Ltda,

Centro de Formação de Condutores Vitória Ltda, and LC Auto Group LLC, I have come to understand that true entrepreneurial freedom comes when a business is capable of operating autonomously, without relying solely on the entrepreneur for every decision or action.

With the accumulated experience, I realized that many entrepreneurs live in a constant cycle of problem-solving and putting out fires. This leads to burnout and prevents them from dedicating time to strategic growth and innovation. I believe that with simplified and well-structured management, it is possible to transform this reality and create businesses that are self-sustaining and prosperous in the long term.

My intention with this book is to share the lessons learned throughout my journey, to demonstrate that management can indeed be simplified, and to help other entrepreneurs build businesses that function autonomously. I believe that with the right tools and strategies, you can transform your business and your life, achieving the freedom you have always sought.

Introduction

Claudio Pinho Junior

When we think about entrepreneurship, the first image that comes to mind is one of freedom: the ability to control our own destiny, set our own schedules, and make decisions autonomously. However, for many entrepreneurs, the reality ends up being an exhausting routine where everything seems to depend exclusively on them. But it doesn't have to be this way. Throughout my career, I discovered that the path to true entrepreneurial freedom lies in building self-managed businesses, where clear processes, a skilled team, and a solid culture enable the company to operate independently.

A self-managed business is one that continues to run successfully, even when the founder is not involved in every detail. This means empowering your team to make decisions, establishing effective management systems, and creating an organizational culture that values autonomy and accountability. When the company becomes less dependent on the entrepreneur, they can focus on what truly matters: innovating, exploring new growth opportunities, and, why not, enjoying more moments with family and friends.

I wrote this book because I believe many entrepreneurs are trapped in a routine where they are constantly drained by operational demands. This is a reality that can be changed. Over the course of my journey, I managed to transform my businesses to make them less reliant on me, which not only reduced my workload but also brought growth and sustainability to the companies.

With this guide, I want to show that it is possible to structure a business that operates autonomously while still being capable of sustainable growth. The practices I share here are the result of years of experience in various sectors, from traffic education to the automotive trade, and represent strategies that truly work. This book is not just a theoretical manual; it offers a practical approach that can be applied immediately to transform the way you manage your business.

This guide is structured to be a practical and straightforward tool. Each chapter addresses a fundamental aspect of building a self-managed business, with real examples, practical tips, and exercises that you can apply to your company. The reading does not need to be linear; you can start with the topic that best fits your current needs and apply the guidance directly to your business.

The idea is for you to use this book as a resource to transform the way you manage your company, making it more efficient and less dependent on you. As you put the strategies presented here into practice, you will see that it is possible to reach a new level of entrepreneurial freedom and make the most of the rewards of your hard work.

I invite you to engage in this journey, to transform your business, and to discover that it is indeed possible to simplify management without losing sight of excellence and sustainable growth.

Chapter 1

Architecting Your Self-Managed Business

"The best way to predict the future is to create it." - Peter Drucker

The dream of many entrepreneurs is to have a business that runs autonomously, allowing them to dedicate their time to innovation, growth, and, of course, quality of life. However, the reality for many is quite the opposite: a routine where they are trapped in daily operations, dealing with urgent problems and activities that consume much of their time and energy. This chapter is about breaking that cycle and architecting a company that is capable of functioning independently, with clear processes and a well-trained team that can take on responsibilities.

Entrepreneurs Trapped in Daily Operations

Many entrepreneurs start their businesses with enthusiasm and a vision of freedom, but they end up becoming the main person responsible for all operational aspects, from customer service to financial management. This creates a situation where the business depends solely on the owner to function, making it vulnerable and limiting its growth potential. Daily operations turn into a vicious cycle, where so much time is spent "putting out fires" that there is no time left to think strategically or invest in innovation.

I personally experienced this situation. In the beginning, I believed that for the business to succeed, I needed to be involved in every detail. However, this only increased my stress level and prevented me from expanding my companies. It was only when I began to implement practices that allowed the business to operate without me that I managed to break this cycle and build companies that grew sustainably.

Defining a Clear Vision for a Self-Managed Business

To start architecting a self-managed business, the first step is to have a clear vision of how this ideal company should function. Ask yourself: If I could be away for three months, what would need to be running perfectly for the business to continue growing without me? This reflection helps identify the critical aspects that need to be automated or delegated.

My experience has shown me that defining a clear vision is essential for guiding the transition from the current model to a self-managed model. This vision is not just an abstract goal but a direction that guides actions, decisions, and the development of internal processes.

Think about the main pillars of your business, such as operations, customer service, marketing, sales, and finance. Imagine how each of these areas would ideally function without your direct supervision. This clarity is the starting point for planning the necessary changes and beginning to architect the processes and systems that will make the business more independent.

Identifying Key Processes for Automation

With the vision established, it's time to analyze daily operations and identify the key processes that can be automated or simplified. Automation does not mean eliminating oversight or neglecting the human touch, but rather reducing the time spent on repetitive and administrative tasks so that you and your team can focus on strategic activities.

Examples of processes that can be automated include:

Financial management: Use accounting software to automate report generation, invoicing, and cash flow control.

Digital marketing: Implement automation tools for scheduling social media posts and email marketing campaigns.

Customer service: Use chatbots to answer common questions and CRM tools to manage customer relationships.

By automating these tasks, you reduce the manual workload and increase efficiency, creating more room for innovation and growth.

Creating a Transition Plan

Creating a self-managed business does not happen overnight. It requires a transition plan that includes steps for the gradual implementation of changes. An effective transition plan should consider the following points:

Prioritize critical processes: Identify the areas that consume the most time and energy and start working on those issues. For example, if financial management takes up much of your day, this may be a priority area for implementing automation solutions.

Delegate responsibilities: Empower your team to take on functions that were previously your responsibility. To do this, invest in training and provide the necessary tools so they can perform their tasks with autonomy and confidence.

Monitor and adjust: Establish performance indicators that allow you to track the progress of changes and make adjustments as needed. Transition is a continuous process, and feedback from the team and customers is essential to ensure that the new practices are delivering the expected results.

By consistently implementing this plan, you will be taking the first steps towards transforming your business into a self-managed company.

Practical Exercise: Starting to Architect Your Self-Managed Business

1. Define Your Vision: Write down how you would like your business to function without your direct intervention. Identify the critical areas and the expected outcomes for each.

2. Identify Three Processes for Automation or Delegation: List three activities that consume a lot of your time and that can be automated or delegated to the team. Note how this change could be implemented.

3. Develop an Action Plan: Create a simple plan to implement the changes identified. Set goals for the next three months, defining weekly tasks that lead to continuous progress.

Claudio Pinho Junior

Chapter 2

The Power of Efficient Processes

Claudio Pinho Junior

"The secret of success is constancy of purpose." - **Benjamin Disraeli**

For a company to become self-managed, it is essential that its processes are efficient and consistent. Poorly defined processes lead to problems such as rework, resource waste, and low productivity, making it difficult for the business to scale. Companies facing these challenges often encounter obstacles in maintaining quality and efficiency as they grow. In this chapter, we will discuss how to map existing processes, identify and eliminate bottlenecks, and standardize operations to achieve the operational efficiency needed for a sustainable business.

Inconsistent and Inefficient Processes

One of the biggest obstacles to business efficiency is the lack of consistency in internal processes. When different team members perform the same task in different ways, the result is variability in service quality, frequent errors, and slower operations. Inconsistent processes negatively affect the customer experience and limit the company's ability to grow and adapt to new demands. Without clear standards, the business ends up relying excessively on improvised practices, losing the opportunity to optimize and streamline operations.

Mapping Existing Processes

To improve process efficiency, the first step is to map them. Process mapping involves visually representing all the steps of an activity or workflow, detailing the tasks performed, the people responsible for each step, and the resources needed. This practice helps to visualize the workflow as a whole, making it easier to identify problems and inefficiencies.

To start, choose a process that directly impacts the company's operation, such as customer service, order management, or financial administration. When mapping the steps, it is important to specify who performs each task, what tools are used, and what decision points may influence the process flow. This initial mapping exercise provides a clear view of operations and helps identify areas that need improvement.

Identifying and Eliminating Bottlenecks

With the process mapping in hand, the next step is to locate the bottlenecks, which are the points that cause delays, rework, or consume resources inefficiently. Identifying these bottlenecks is essential to guide optimization efforts, as these steps are usually the main culprits for slow and inconsistent processes.

To identify bottlenecks, ask the following questions:

- Which steps in the process are the most time-consuming?
- Are there manual approval dependencies that could be simplified or automated?
- At which points do errors occur most frequently?

- Are there activities that require frequent rework or repetition?

Once bottlenecks are identified, think of ways to reduce or eliminate them. This can be done by automating routine tasks, redistributing responsibilities, or simplifying steps that do not add value to the process. Eliminating bottlenecks helps free up time and resources that can be invested in strategic activities.

Standardizing and Documenting Processes

After eliminating bottlenecks and simplifying the workflow, it is time to standardize the processes. Standardization involves defining consistent practices and methods for task execution so that the entire team follows the same guidelines. This ensures that results are predictable and of high quality, regardless of who is performing the activity.

Documenting the standardized processes is crucial to ensuring that the team has a reference guide for carrying out tasks. This may include manuals, checklists, and flowcharts that describe each step of the process and the resources needed. Documentation facilitates the training of new employees and serves as a resource for the team, ensuring that everyone follows the same procedures.

Standardizing and documenting processes is also essential for business scalability, allowing the company to grow without losing consistency and quality in its services or products. A well-documented process helps maintain operational efficiency and provides a solid foundation for continuous improvement.

Practical Exercise: Optimizing Your Processes

1. Map a Critical Process: Choose a process relevant to the business, such as sales, customer service, or logistics. Draw a flowchart representing each step,

identifying who performs each task, what tools are used, and where the critical points are.

2. **Identify Bottlenecks and Suggest Improvements:** Analyze the mapping and identify bottlenecks that are causing delays or inefficiencies. Describe each bottleneck and suggest at least one solution to resolve it.

3. **Create a Standard Document for the Process:** With the proposed improvements, develop a document that standardizes the process. Include detailed guidelines on how to perform each step, which tools to use, and best practices to ensure efficiency.

Chapter 3

The Art of Effective Delegation

Claudio Pinho Junior

"No man will make a great business who wants to do it all himself or get all the credit." - Andrew Carnegie

Effective delegation is an essential skill for any entrepreneur who wants to build a self-managed business. When responsibilities are not distributed properly, the entrepreneur ends up overwhelmed and stuck with operational tasks, hindering growth and preventing a focus on long-term strategies. Delegating is not just about transferring tasks to others, but rather trusting the team to take on responsibilities and make decisions that contribute to the business's success.

In this chapter, we will explore how to identify tasks that can be delegated, develop an efficient structure for delegation, and overcome the fear of losing control when transferring responsibilities to others.

Difficulty Delegating Responsibilities

One of the greatest barriers to effective delegation is the difficulty in trusting that others can perform certain tasks with the same quality and attention to detail as the entrepreneur. This often leads to micromanagement, where the business owner tries to closely supervise all activities, resulting in burnout and limiting the team's autonomy. This approach not only exhausts the entrepreneur but also stifles the development of employees, who end up without opportunities to grow and take on new challenges.

Overcoming this difficulty is crucial for building a company that operates autonomously and efficiently. Proper delegation can free up time and energy for the entrepreneur to focus on strategic initiatives and business growth.

Identifying Delegable Tasks

The first step in effective delegation is identifying tasks that can be transferred to others. These tasks often include repetitive, administrative, or operational activities that take up a large portion of time and do not necessarily require the entrepreneur's involvement. To determine which tasks are suitable for delegation, consider the following criteria:

Frequency: Recurring and routine tasks are ideal for delegation, as they can be performed with proper training and well-defined procedures.

Complexity: Activities that do not require specialized skills or in-depth business knowledge can be easily delegated. Even more complex tasks can be delegated if the employee receives the necessary training.

Strategic Impact: If the task does not significantly impact strategic business decisions, it is a strong candidate for delegation. The entrepreneur should focus efforts on activities that truly add value to the company.

Creating a list of tasks that meet these criteria can be a starting point for distributing responsibilities and alleviating the workload.

Developing a Delegation Structure

For delegation to be effective, it is necessary to develop a well-defined structure that ensures responsibilities are transferred clearly and that employees have the tools and knowledge needed to carry them out. This structure should include:

Definition of Roles and Responsibilities: Clearly establish who is responsible for which tasks, and ensure all team members understand their roles. This helps prevent overlap and ensures that each employee knows what is expected of them.

Creation of Standard Procedures: Document processes so that employees can follow clear instructions on how to perform delegated tasks. This facilitates training and reduces the margin for error.

Establishment of Deadlines and Goals: When delegating a task, set realistic deadlines and goals that allow for performance measurement. This provides a clear benchmark for evaluating whether the task was successfully executed.

Feedback and Adjustments: Monitor the team's performance and provide regular feedback. This is important for fine-tuning the approach and ensuring expectations are being met. Delegation should not be a static process; it needs to be adjusted based on needs and performance.

Overcoming the Fear of Losing Control

The fear of losing control is one of the main reasons why many entrepreneurs avoid delegating. To overcome this fear, it is essential to change the mindset regarding delegation, seeing it as an opportunity to develop and empower the team rather than as a risk of losing control over the business.

Here are some strategies to overcome this fear:

Start Small: Delegate small tasks initially and gradually increase the complexity of the responsibilities transferred as you and your team become more comfortable.

Trust the Process: Remember that the delegation structure was developed to ensure tasks are carried out according to defined standards. Trust that, with proper training and clear procedures, the team will be able to meet expectations.

Accept That Mistakes May Happen: Mistakes are part of the learning process. It is important to view errors as learning opportunities and adjust procedures as needed.

By following these strategies, delegation becomes more natural, and the benefits of having a more skilled and autonomous team become evident.

Practical Exercise: Implementing Effective Delegation

1. Identify Three Tasks to Delegate: Make a list of three activities that take up much of your time and can be delegated to an employee. Note why each task is suitable for delegation.

2. Develop a Delegation Plan for Each Task: For each identified task, create a delegation plan that includes who will be responsible, how the task will be performed (instructions or procedures), deadlines for completion, and performance metrics.

3. Monitor and Adjust: After delegating the tasks, monitor the progress and provide feedback to the team. If necessary, adjust the instructions and procedures to improve execution.

Claudio Pinho Junior

Chapter 4

Automating for Success

Claudio Pinho Junior

"Technology is just a tool. To help kids work together, the important thing is motivation." - Bill Gates

Automation is one of the most effective ways to reduce the time and resources spent on manual processes. When repetitive and administrative tasks are performed manually, business efficiency is compromised, and the team loses time that could be dedicated to strategic and high-value activities. Process automation allows the company to operate more agilely and scalably, eliminating the need for manual interventions and reducing the margin for error.

Manual Processes Consuming Time and Resources

Manual processes not only consume time but are also prone to human error. As the business grows, dependence on manual procedures becomes increasingly detrimental, resulting in delays and a growing demand for resources to handle operational tasks. Furthermore, processes that are not automated make it difficult to monitor and measure performance, as data collection and analysis become more complex and time-consuming.

Overcoming these challenges requires adopting technologies that automate workflows, increase efficiency, and provide a clearer view of the business.

Evaluating Automation Tools

The first step in automating processes is evaluating which tools are suitable for the specific needs of the business. There are many automation solutions available in the market, from financial management software and digital marketing tools to customer service platforms. The choice of the right tools should consider the following factors:

Functionality: Evaluate whether the tool meets the specific needs of your business, such as sales management, payment processing, inventory control, or marketing campaign execution.

Integration: Check if the tool can be integrated with existing systems, such as CRM, accounting, or ERP software. Integration prevents data duplication and improves the fluidity of operations.

Scalability: Ensure that the chosen solution can be expanded to keep pace with business growth. A tool that works well for a small company may not meet the demands of an expanding operation.

Conducting detailed research on the available options and testing some tools with a sample of users can help choose the best solution for the business.

Implementing Integrated Systems

Once the tools are selected, it is essential to implement integrated systems that connect all areas of the business, allowing data to flow continuously between departments. For example, integrating a sales system with accounting software can automate the issuance of invoices and cash flow control, saving time and reducing the risk of errors.

Implementing integrated systems provides a holistic view of the business, where information can be accessed in real-time for decision-making. This practice also improves communication among teams, who gain access to the same information, facilitating collaboration and alignment.

To ensure successful implementation, follow these steps:

Plan the Integration: Define which systems will be connected and how data will be shared between them. Create an implementation schedule to ensure a smooth transition.

Test the Configuration: Before launching the systems, conduct tests to ensure that everything functions as expected and that the data is transferred correctly.

Adjust as Needed: During the implementation, additional needs or problems may arise that require adjustments. Be flexible and adapt the system configuration to resolve these issues.

Training the Team in New Technologies

Automation will only be effective if the team is prepared to use the new technologies. It is essential that all employees understand the tools and know how to use them to enhance their performance. Training is a fundamental part of this process, ensuring that the team adopts automation effectively and maximizes the benefits provided by the new technologies.

When implementing training, consider the following points:

Hands-On Training Sessions: Provide opportunities for employees to practice using the tools during training. This helps consolidate learning and facilitates the transition to the new systems.

Ongoing Support: Offer continuous support to employees after the initial training, ensuring they can clarify doubts and solve problems quickly.

Feedback: Collect feedback from the team regarding the use of the new technologies to identify areas that can be improved and adjust the training as needed.

Proper training is what turns automation into a competitive advantage, ensuring that the team feels confident and prepared to use the systems effectively.

Practical Exercise: Starting Automation in Your Business

1. Identify Three Manual Processes for Automation: List three activities that are currently performed

manually and consume a lot of time. Describe why these activities are suitable for automation.

2. Research Tools to Automate Each Process: For each identified process, research two or three tools that can be used to automate it. Note the functionalities of each tool, its cost, and possible integrations with other systems in your company.

3. Develop a Training Plan for the Team: Create a plan to train the team in using the new tools. Include the training format (in-person, online, etc.), duration, and the support materials that will be needed to help employees adapt.

Claudio Pinho Junior

Chapter 5

Measuring Success: KPIs That Matter

Claudio Pinho Junior

"What gets measured, gets managed." - Peter Drucker

For a business to become self-managed and sustainable, it is essential to continuously measure its performance. Without clear metrics, it is impossible to evaluate progress, identify problems, or make informed decisions. Key Performance Indicators (KPIs) are fundamental tools for monitoring the most important aspects of a business and guiding its growth. However, many entrepreneurs struggle to define which KPIs are most relevant to their operations and to implement an effective monitoring system.

Lack of Clear Metrics to Evaluate Performance

When a business does not measure its performance adequately, managers have no way of knowing whether goals are being met or if there are areas that need adjustment. Without clear indicators, it is difficult to identify weaknesses and opportunities for improvement, which can result in decisions based on assumptions or incomplete information. This lack of data-driven insights can compromise growth and business efficiency.

Implementing KPIs allows you to track progress objectively and take proactive measures to address problems or explore new opportunities. To do so, it is necessary to choose the right indicators and monitor them consistently.

Identifying Critical KPIs for the Business

The most relevant KPIs vary depending on the sector and the company's objectives. To identify the most critical indicators, it is important to understand which metrics directly reflect the success and health of the business. When choosing KPIs, consider the following aspects:

Financial: Indicators such as revenue, profit margins, cash flow, and operating costs are essential for monitoring financial health.

Operational: Metrics related to process efficiency, such as cycle time, productivity, and error rates, help assess operational effectiveness.

Customers: Indicators such as customer satisfaction, retention rate, and Net Promoter Score (NPS) are useful for measuring the quality of service and customer loyalty.

Marketing and Sales: KPIs such as customer acquisition cost (CAC), conversion rate, and return on investment (ROI) in campaigns are critical for evaluating the effectiveness of marketing and sales strategies.

The choice of KPIs should be aligned with the business's strategic objectives so that the indicators provide useful information to guide decisions.

Implementing Monitoring Systems

After defining the critical KPIs, the next step is to implement monitoring systems that allow for continuous and automated tracking of the indicators. There are many tools available on the market that help collect, organize, and analyze performance data, such as CRM software, marketing analytics platforms, and ERP systems.

To ensure effective monitoring, follow these steps:

Automate Data Collection: Whenever possible, automate the data collection process to reduce errors and ensure that information is always up-to-date.

Establish Monitoring Frequency: Determine how often the KPIs will be reviewed (daily, weekly, monthly). The frequency will depend on the nature of the indicator and the sector.

Use Visual Dashboards: Dashboards are useful for visualizing KPIs clearly and objectively. They allow you to track performance in real-time and make it easier to identify trends or anomalies.

Implementing monitoring systems enables data to be analyzed quickly and consistently, providing valuable insights for business management.

Using Data to Make Decisions

The data collected through KPIs is a powerful tool for making strategic and operational decisions. However, it is essential to interpret the data correctly and use it to guide specific actions. To do this, consider the following practices:

Trend Analysis: Evaluate trends in KPIs over time to identify patterns, such as sales peaks during certain periods or an increase in the error rate in a specific process.

Comparison with Goals: Compare KPI results with established goals to assess performance and determine if corrective actions are needed.

Evidence-Based Decisions: Use the data to make informed decisions, avoiding relying solely on intuition or perceptions. For example, if the customer satisfaction KPI is declining, a deeper analysis of the data can reveal specific areas where service needs improvement.

Effectively using KPIs allows the entrepreneur to adopt a proactive approach to business management, anticipating problems and seizing growth opportunities.

Practical Exercise: Implementing KPIs in Your Business

1. Define Three Relevant KPIs for Your Business: Choose three KPIs that are critical for monitoring your company's performance. Consider financial, operational, and customer satisfaction aspects.

2. Set Goals for Each KPI: Establish specific goals for the selected KPIs. The goals should be measurable and realistic, with clear deadlines for achievement.

3. **Set Up a Monitoring System:** Select a tool to monitor the KPIs and configure a dashboard that allows you to visualize the results. Establish a frequency for reviewing the data and adjusting the goals as needed.

Claudio Pinho Junior

Chapter 6

Leading from a Distance

Claudio Pinho Junior

"Leadership is the capacity to translate vision into reality."
- Warren Bennis

Managing remote teams has become an increasingly common reality in the business world. With technological advancements and the growing trend toward remote work, leading teams effectively requires new approaches and skills. While managing remote teams offers benefits such as greater flexibility and global reach, it also presents challenges, such as maintaining efficient communication, building trust, and ensuring collaboration among team members who may be geographically dispersed.

Managing Remote Teams Effectively

Managing teams that work remotely can be challenging, especially when it comes to ensuring that everyone is on the same page, maintaining productivity, and staying aligned with business objectives. The lack of in-person interactions can make communication difficult and reduce team cohesion. Additionally, remote work can lead to employee isolation, which can harm morale and engagement. Overcoming these challenges requires a conscious effort to create a virtual work environment that facilitates collaboration and effective communication.

Establishing Communication Protocols

For a remote team to function efficiently, it is crucial to define clear communication protocols. This means setting rules and guidelines about how and when communication should occur, which tools will be used, and what the expectations are regarding response times and availability.

Some practices for establishing effective protocols include:

Defining Communication Channels: Use different channels for different types of communication. For example, use email for formal communications, chat for quick interactions, and video conferencing for more complex meetings or project discussions.

Establishing Meeting Frequency: Determine the frequency of team meetings, whether daily, weekly, or monthly, depending on project needs. Regular check-in meetings help keep the team connected and informed about task progress.

Creating Standards for Information Sharing: Ensure that everyone knows where documents, reports, and other essential information are stored and how to access them. This prevents important information from being lost or overlooked.

Defining these protocols helps keep communication fluid and avoids misunderstandings, allowing all team members to know exactly what is expected of them.

Building Trust in Virtual Environments

Building trust within remote teams is essential for ensuring collaboration and engagement. In physical environments, trust is often built through spontaneous interactions and informal contacts. In a remote setting, specific approaches are needed to create a positive work atmosphere.

Strategies for building trust in virtual environments include:

Encouraging Transparency: Open and transparent communication about project progress, challenges, and expectations helps create an environment of trust. Make sure all team members feel comfortable sharing their opinions and providing feedback.

Recognizing and Valuing Contributions: Celebrate achievements and recognize employees' efforts. Public recognition, such as praise during meetings or thank-you messages, reinforces a sense of belonging and appreciation.

Establishing Personal Connections: Promote activities that allow team members to get to know each other better, even at a distance. Informal moments during meetings, such as brief "icebreakers" or casual conversations, help strengthen bonds and create a more cohesive team.

These practices create a culture of trust and collaboration, even without the physical presence of team members.

Utilizing Remote Collaboration Tools

The use of remote collaboration tools is essential for maintaining productivity and ensuring that all team members have access to the information they need. There are many tools available that facilitate collaborative work, from video conferencing platforms to project management software.

When choosing the right tools, consider the following aspects:

Ease of Use: The tools should be intuitive and easy to use so that everyone can adopt them quickly.

Integration with Other Systems: Make sure the chosen tools can be integrated with other systems the team already uses, such as CRM, ERP, or marketing automation software.

Required Features: Evaluate the features offered by the tools, such as file sharing, real-time communication, video conferencing, and task management. Choose those that best meet the business's specific needs.

Tools like Slack, Microsoft Teams, Zoom, Trello, Asana, and Google Workspace are commonly used to maintain fluid collaboration and communication in remote teams. Choosing the right tool can have a significant impact on work efficiency.

Practical Exercise: Improving Remote Leadership

1. Develop a Communication Protocol: Create a plan for your remote team's communication protocols, including which channels will be used, the frequency of meetings, and standards for sharing information.

2. Plan a Trust-Building Activity: Organize a virtual activity to promote relationships among team members, such as an icebreaker session during a meeting, an online game, or an informal collaborative activity.

3. Evaluate the Collaboration Tools Used by the Team: Make a list of the collaboration tools your team currently uses and assess whether they meet the needs. Identify at least one new tool that could improve efficiency and make a plan to test it.

Claudio Pinho Junior

Chapter 7

Cultivating Autonomy in the Team

Claudio Pinho Junior

"Treat people as if they were what they ought to be, and you help them become what they are capable of being."
- Johann Wolfgang von Goethe

Team autonomy is one of the fundamental pillars for creating a self-managed business. When employees are empowered to make decisions and solve problems on their own, the entrepreneur can focus on strategic issues rather than being stuck in micromanagement. However, many teams develop a culture of dependency, where members wait for detailed instructions or approval for every decision, limiting efficiency and proactivity.

A Team Dependent on Micromanagement

Micromanagement occurs when leaders closely oversee every task, reviewing details and making decisions that could be delegated to employees. This practice not only overburdens the manager but also stifles creativity and team development, creating excessive dependency. To break this cycle, it is necessary to promote autonomy by empowering employees to take responsibility and initiative.

Developing a Culture of Responsibility

To cultivate team autonomy, the first step is to establish a culture of responsibility, where everyone is encouraged to take ownership of their tasks and decisions. This involves setting clear expectations about what is expected from each team member and creating an environment where mistakes are seen as learning opportunities, not grounds for punishment.

Some practices for developing a culture of responsibility include:

Setting Clear Goals: Define specific and measurable goals for the team and individuals, making it clear how each person contributes to the overall success of the business. This gives employees a clear view of the impact of their actions.

Encouraging Decision-Making: Empower team members to make decisions within their areas of responsibility, providing guidelines so they can evaluate options with confidence. This increases the sense of ownership and accountability for the results.

Reinforcing Ownership of Outcomes: Celebrate the successes achieved by the team and openly discuss mistakes. Encouraging employees to reflect on the outcomes helps promote learning and continuous improvement.

Responsibility should be seen as a natural part of the team's routine, where each employee understands their role and continuously strives for excellence.

Implementing Mentoring Programs

Mentoring is a powerful tool for developing autonomy, as it allows employees to learn directly from experienced leaders, acquiring the skills and confidence needed to take on new responsibilities. Implementing a formal mentoring program can accelerate team members' development and prepare future leaders.

To create an effective mentoring program, follow these steps:

Identify Mentors and Mentees: Choose experienced professionals who can share their knowledge and team members who wish to grow and assume more responsibilities. The alignment between mentor and mentee is essential for the program's success.

Set Goals for the Mentorship: Clearly define what the participants are expected to achieve through mentoring. This may include developing specific skills, preparing for new challenges, or improving leadership competencies.

Create a Follow-Up Plan: Ensure that meetings between mentors and mentees are regular and that progress is monitored. Provide guidance and resources to help mentors offer effective support.

A well-structured mentoring program not only strengthens the team's skills but also creates a culture of continuous development, where learning is valued and encouraged.

Providing Growth Opportunities

To motivate the team to take on more responsibilities, it is essential to have clear and accessible growth opportunities. When employees see a path for career advancement, they are more inclined to dedicate themselves and pursue improvement.

Some ways to offer these opportunities include:

Continuous Professional Development: Promote training, workshops, and courses that allow employees to acquire new skills and improve existing competencies.

Job Rotation: Provide opportunities for team members to experience different roles or departments, broadening their understanding of the business and increasing their adaptability.

Career Plans: Create structured career plans that clearly show how employees can grow within the company. This helps align expectations and motivates the team to strive for new achievements.

Growth opportunities should be integrated into the company's culture so that everyone knows that continuous development is a priority and a real possibility.

Practical Exercise: Fostering Autonomy in Your Team

1. Set Three Goals to Promote Responsibility: Create three clear goals to encourage responsibility in your team, specifying expectations and how success will be measured.

2. Develop a Mentoring Program: Draft a basic plan for implementing a mentoring program in your company, identifying potential mentors and mentees, as well as the program's objectives.

3. Create a Growth Opportunity Plan: Describe two or three initiatives to offer development opportunities for your team, such as specific training, job rotation, or a structured career plan.

Claudio Pinho Junior

Chapter 8

Building a Championship Team

Claudio Pinho Junior

"Talent wins games, but teamwork and intelligence win championships." - Michael Jordan

Building a high-performance team is essential for any business to achieve success and remain competitive. However, many companies face challenges when trying to attract and retain top talent, especially in a constantly evolving and competitive job market. To form a championship team, it is necessary not only to recruit the right people but also to create an environment that inspires excellence and values continuous development.

Difficulty Attracting and Retaining Top Talent

Finding qualified individuals is only part of the challenge. Once talented people are hired, keeping them motivated and committed over the long term requires a proactive approach to ensure they feel valued and engaged. When there is no clarity about the ideal profiles needed for each role, recruitment processes can become inconsistent and ineffective. Additionally, without an attractive and inclusive work environment, it is difficult to retain top talent and avoid high turnover.

Defining Ideal Profiles for Each Role

To attract the best talent, the first step is to define the ideal profiles for each position within the company. This means understanding not only the required technical skills but also the behavioral competencies and values that align with the organizational culture.

When defining ideal profiles, consider the following aspects:

Technical Skills and Experience: Determine which qualifications are necessary for the role, such as experience with a specific tool, specialized knowledge, or certifications.

Behavioral Competencies: Identify the behavioral characteristics important for the position, which may include teamwork skills, resilience, proactivity, or attention to detail.

Cultural Alignment: Evaluate whether the candidate aligns with the company's values and culture. Cultural fit is essential to ensure that the employee feels integrated and can contribute positively to the work environment.

Defining detailed profiles for each role helps guide the recruitment process and increases the likelihood of finding individuals who truly fit the team.

Implementing Effective Recruitment Processes

A well-structured recruitment process is essential to ensure the hiring of high-performing talent. This requires adopting a systematic approach that goes beyond resume analysis and traditional interviews, incorporating tools and practices that help identify the best candidates.

To implement effective recruitment processes, follow these steps:

Attractive and Clear Job Postings: Create detailed and appealing job descriptions, highlighting the benefits of working at the company, expectations for the position, and the impact the employee will have. This helps attract candidates who align with the role's objectives.

Varied Selection Techniques: Use a combination of techniques to evaluate candidates, such as behavioral interviews, technical tests, and group dynamics. This allows for a more comprehensive assessment of skills and potential.

Structured Interviews: Adopt a structured interview format with predefined questions to assess specific competencies and alignment with the company's values. This ensures that all candidates are evaluated consistently.

Using well-defined recruitment processes not only improves the quality of hires but also provides a positive experience for the candidates.

Creating an Environment That Attracts Top Talent

Attracting and retaining top talent goes beyond competitive salaries or benefits. It is necessary to create a work environment that inspires employees to give their best, providing growth opportunities and promoting a culture of recognition.

Some practices for creating an attractive environment include:

Development and Growth Opportunities: Offer training programs, coaching, and career plans that allow employees to grow within the company. This demonstrates that the organization invests in their development and cares about their future.

Recognition and Reward Programs: Value the team's achievements and outstanding performance.

Non-monetary recognition programs, such as awards, public praise, and additional time off, can be effective in motivating employees.

Inclusive and Open Culture: Promote an environment where all opinions are respected, and employees feel comfortable sharing ideas and suggesting improvements. The diversity of thoughts and experiences enriches the organization and contributes to a positive work atmosphere.

These initiatives help create a company where top talent wants to work, while also promoting engagement and satisfaction among existing employees.

Practical Exercise: Building a High-Performance Team

1. Define the Ideal Profile for a Specific Role: Choose a role within the company and describe the ideal profile, considering the necessary technical skills, behavioral competencies, and cultural alignment.

2. Review the Current Recruitment Process: Analyze the company's existing recruitment process and identify three areas that could be improved. Propose changes that could be implemented to make it more effective.

3. Develop an Initiative to Improve the Work Environment: Plan a specific action to create a more attractive environment for employees, such as implementing a recognition program or organizing professional development activities.

Claudio Pinho Junior

Chapter 9

Mastering Time for Leaders

Claudio Pinho Junior

"Time is the scarcest resource, and unless it is managed, nothing else can be managed." - Peter Drucker

Effective time management is one of the greatest challenges faced by leaders and entrepreneurs. With multiple daily demands, from supervising teams to developing long-term strategies, it's easy to feel overwhelmed and lose focus on what truly matters. To achieve high-level performance, it is essential to master the art of managing time efficiently, prioritizing tasks, establishing productive routines, and eliminating time-wasters.

Ineffective Time Management for Leaders

Leaders often struggle with an overload of tasks and responsibilities, leading to ineffective time management. When everything seems urgent, important tasks end up being overlooked, and priorities become confusing. This lack of clarity on where to focus efforts can reduce productivity and cause stress. Furthermore, poor organization results in wasted time on non-essential or irrelevant tasks, diverting the leader's attention from strategic issues that require focus.

Task Prioritization Techniques

Prioritizing tasks is crucial for effective time management. Several techniques can be used to determine which tasks should be addressed first, based on their importance and urgency.

Some of the most effective techniques include:

Eisenhower Matrix: Also known as the urgent/important matrix, this technique helps categorize tasks into four quadrants:

- Urgent and Important (must be done immediately).

- Important but Not Urgent (should be planned for later).
- Urgent but Not Important (should be delegated).
- Neither Urgent Nor Important (should be postponed or eliminated).

80/20 Rule (Pareto Principle): This technique suggests that 20% of activities generate 80% of results. Identify which tasks have the most impact and focus on them. The goal is to eliminate or reduce time spent on activities that do not add significant value.

ABCDE Method: Classify daily tasks into five categories according to their importance:

A: Tasks that must be done, as they have major consequences.

B: Tasks that should be done, but with smaller consequences if not completed.

C: Tasks that would be nice to do but are not essential.

D: Tasks that can be delegated to someone else.

E: Tasks that can be eliminated without impact.

These techniques help keep focus on the tasks that truly matter, ensuring that time is used more efficiently.

Implementing Productive Routines

Well-established routines are crucial for maintaining productivity and avoiding distractions. Creating a daily ritual that includes specific times for planning, executing priority tasks, and reviewing progress can significantly increase efficiency. To implement productive routines, consider the following suggestions:

Plan the Day in Advance: Before ending the workday, set aside a few minutes to plan for the next day. This includes identifying the most important tasks to be accomplished and creating a priority list.

Time Blocking: Organize the day into blocks of time dedicated to specific tasks, such as meetings, focused work, or problem-solving. This helps prevent fragmentation and keeps focus on one activity at a time.

Weekly Reviews: Set aside time each week to review what was accomplished, assess progress towards goals, and adjust plans for the upcoming weeks. Reviews help identify areas for improvement and reprioritize as necessary.

Consistent routines provide a structure that facilitates the execution of important tasks and creates a sustainable work rhythm.

Eliminating Time-Wasters

Time-wasters are activities that consume energy and attention but add no value to the business. Identifying and eliminating these distractions is essential to freeing up more time for what truly matters. Some common time-wasters include:

Ineffective Meetings: Avoid meetings without a clear agenda or specific purpose. Whenever possible, replace long meetings with quick calls or emails, and limit the duration to ensure objectivity.

Constant Interruptions: Minimize distractions such as email notifications and instant messages. Set specific times to check communications rather than interrupting work constantly.

Multitasking: Avoid trying to handle multiple tasks simultaneously. Focus on one activity at a time to ensure it is completed with quality and efficiency.

Reducing or eliminating these time-consuming activities frees the leader to focus on more important and strategic matters.

Practical Exercise: Improving Time Management

1. Apply the Eisenhower Matrix to Your Current Tasks: Make a list of tasks that need to be done and classify them using the Eisenhower

Matrix. Identify which should be done immediately, which can be scheduled for later, what can be delegated, and what can be eliminated.

2. Create a Daily Time-Blocking Routine: Organize your day into blocks of time dedicated to different types of activities (focused work, meetings, planning). Try this routine for a week and evaluate the results.

3. Identify Three Time-Wasters and Make a Plan to Eliminate Them: List three activities that consume a lot of your time and develop strategies to minimize or eliminate them.

Claudio Pinho Junior

Chapter 10

Agility in Business

Claudio Pinho Junior

"It is not the strongest of the species that survive, nor the most intelligent, but the one most adaptable to change."
- Charles Darwin

In today's business landscape, the ability to adapt is essential for survival and growth. Organizational rigidity and inflexible processes can slow a company down, making it unable to respond swiftly to market changes. In an environment of constant transformations, adopting an agile approach can provide the necessary flexibility to face challenges and seize new opportunities.

Organizational Rigidity in a Rapidly Changing World

Organizational rigidity occurs when a company's processes and structures are inflexible, making it difficult to respond quickly to changes in the external environment. This can lead to missed opportunities, delays in delivering products or services, and difficulty staying relevant in the market. Companies operating with traditional management models often struggle to adapt to new demands, as processes are linear and changes are slow.

Organizational agility, on the other hand, allows companies to adapt quickly, be proactive regarding changes, and maintain efficiency. This requires adopting practices that prioritize flexibility and continuous improvement.

Implementing Agile Methodologies in Management

Agile methodologies are approaches to project and process management that focus on rapid deliveries, constant feedback, and adaptation to change. Originally developed for the software industry, these methodologies can be applied in any sector to increase efficiency and adaptability.

Some principles of agile methodologies include:

Short, Incremental Iterations: Instead of planning an entire project at once, break it down into small steps or sprints. This allows the team to deliver results quickly and make adjustments as needed.

Task Prioritization: Focus on activities that generate the most value for the customer and the business. Reassess priorities regularly to ensure the team is always working on the most relevant tasks.

Team Autonomy: Encourage self-organization and collaboration, allowing teams to make quick decisions and adapt to changes more easily.

Implementing agile methodologies in management promotes greater dynamism and enables companies to respond quickly to market needs.

Creating Rapid Feedback Cycles

Rapid feedback cycles are essential for adjusting processes, products, and services based on updated information and user or customer experience. By obtaining constant feedback, the company can identify problems quickly and adjust its strategies before they escalate.

To create effective feedback cycles, consider the following practices:

Review and Retrospective Meetings: Conduct regular reviews to discuss what went well and what can be improved in each project or sprint. This enables quick and ongoing adjustments.

Customer Feedback: Frequently collect feedback from customers, through surveys, interviews, or behavior analysis. Use this information to guide the development of products and services.

Real-Time Data Analysis: Utilize data analysis tools to monitor performance and identify emerging trends. This helps adjust strategies based on evidence rather than assumptions.

Rapid feedback cycles provide a proactive approach to continuous improvement, keeping the company aligned with market needs.

Fostering a Culture of Continuous Innovation

Business agility requires a culture of innovation that encourages creativity and experimentation. To maintain this mindset, it is important to create an environment where the pursuit of new ideas is encouraged and mistakes are seen as part of the learning process.

Strategies to foster continuous innovation include:

Encouraging Experimentation: Allow teams to test new ideas on a small scale before implementing them broadly. This helps identify viable solutions quickly without committing significant resources.

Ideas and Suggestions Programs: Create mechanisms for all employees to share improvement ideas, and reward those whose suggestions are successfully implemented.

Space for Creative Development: Set aside time for activities that encourage creative thinking, such as hackathons, innovation workshops, or brainstorming sessions.

Promoting a culture of continuous innovation ensures that the organization is always ready to adapt and evolve, staying relevant in a competitive environment.

Practical Exercise: Increasing Agility in Your Business

1. Plan the Implementation of an Agile Sprint: Choose a project or process to implement an agile sprint. Break it down into smaller steps, define the sprint duration (e.g., two weeks), and set clear goals for each step.

2. Create a Feedback Cycle for a Current Project: Select an ongoing project and establish a regular feedback routine, such as weekly review meetings

and customer feedback collection. Make a plan to use this information to improve the project.

3. Launch an Ideas Program in the Team: Develop a suggestions program to encourage the team to present improvement ideas. Establish a way to evaluate and implement the most viable suggestions, and recognize and reward employees.

Claudio Pinho Junior

Chapter 11

Communication That Transforms

Claudio Pinho Junior

"Communication is the ability to ensure that you are understood exactly as you intend." - Jim Rohn

Effective communication is fundamental to the success of any company. It forms the foundation for aligning objectives, executing tasks efficiently, and building a healthy organizational culture. However, communication failures are common in corporate environments and can lead to misunderstandings, errors, loss of productivity, and even conflicts. To transform communication into a powerful tool, it is necessary to establish effective channels, implement rituals that ensure a constant flow of information, and promote a culture of transparency and feedback.

Communication Failures Undermining Efficiency

Ineffective communication can manifest in various forms, such as information not reaching employees, confusing messages, or the absence of appropriate channels for feedback exchange. These failures result in rework, misalignment, and missed opportunities. In many cases, companies do not define clear communication standards, leading to information scatter and increased noise. To overcome this problem, practices must be adopted to ensure that information flows efficiently and that all team members are well-informed.

Establishing Effective Communication Channels

Choosing the right communication channels is essential to ensure that information reaches the intended recipient at the right time and with the necessary clarity. Different types of communication require different channels, depending on the content and target audience. Some practices for establishing effective communication channels include:

Defining Channels for Specific Types of Communication: Use email for formal and long-term communications, instant messaging tools for quick interactions, and video conferencing for detailed discussions or important meetings.

Using Collaborative Platforms: Tools like Slack, Microsoft Teams, or Google Workspace facilitate real-time information exchange and allow integration of different functionalities, such as chat, video conferencing, and file sharing.

Centralizing Important Information: Have a designated location for storing and sharing relevant documents, such as company policies, procedure manuals, and important updates. This can be done through an intranet or a knowledge management platform.

Establishing well-defined channels reduces confusion about where and how information should be shared, ensuring that all employees know where to find what they need.

Implementing Communication Rituals

Communication rituals are regular and standardized practices that ensure a constant flow of information and keep the team aligned. They are especially important in companies where projects are dynamic or teams work remotely or in a hybrid model.

To implement effective communication rituals, consider the following examples:

Daily Stand-Up Meetings: Short meetings, usually 15 minutes, where the team discusses what was done the previous day, what will be done today, and any obstacles. This ensures that everyone is aware of progress and priorities.

Weekly Reviews: Weekly meetings to review goal progress and discuss planning for the coming week. These reviews help identify bottlenecks and adjust planning as needed.

Feedback and Retrospective Meetings: Monthly or quarterly rituals where the team reflects on what worked well and what could be improved. These meetings promote continuous improvement and ensure that the team is always looking for ways to enhance performance.

Established communication rituals promote consistency and help keep the team focused, preventing important information from being lost.

Promoting Transparency and Constant Feedback

Transparency is one of the most important components for creating a healthy organizational culture. When employees have access to relevant information and are aware of decisions made by leadership, trust increases and engagement strengthens. Constant feedback is also essential to ensure that everyone knows how they are performing and where they can improve.

To promote transparency and constant feedback, adopt these practices:

Share Goals and Results: Regularly inform the team about project progress, goal achievement, and results. This can be done through weekly updates or monthly reports.

Encourage Two-Way Feedback: Create channels for employees to give feedback to leadership, as well as receive feedback on their performance. This can be done through climate surveys, feedback sessions, or suggestion boxes.

Recognize and Celebrate Successes: When the team or individuals reach important goals, acknowledge the results publicly. This strengthens the culture of appreciation and reinforces the importance of maintaining clear and open communication.

These practices create a work environment where information is shared honestly, and feedback is seen as a growth tool, not as criticism.

Practical Exercise: Improving Communication in the Company

1. Evaluate Current Communication Channels: Analyze the communication channels currently used in the company and identify areas for improvement. Determine which channels need to be updated or replaced.

2. Implement a Communication Ritual: Choose one of the communication rituals mentioned (daily stand-up, weekly reviews, feedback meetings) and implement it with your team. Define a frequency and format, then evaluate the results after a month.

3. Create a Plan to Increase Transparency: Develop a plan to share information more transparently with the team, such as monthly performance reports or an internal communication board. Include ways to obtain feedback from employees about what is being shared.

Claudio Pinho Junior

Chapter 12

The Future is Now: Staying Ahead

"The best time to plant a tree was 20 years ago. The second-best time is now." - Chinese Proverb

In a world of constant change, keeping a business relevant and competitive requires proactivity and a forward-looking mindset. The inability to quickly adapt to market shifts can lead to obsolescence, while companies that anticipate trends and cultivate a culture of continuous learning stay ahead. In this chapter, we will discuss how to develop a culture of continuous learning, anticipate market changes, and continuously adapt the business model to ensure the company remains competitive in the long term.

Maintaining Business Relevance and Competitiveness Over Time

With the rapid pace of innovation and the evolving preferences of consumers, businesses face the challenge of staying up-to-date and ready to address new market demands. Companies that cling to outdated practices or resist change end up losing ground to more agile and innovative competitors. To avoid stagnation, it is essential to adopt a dynamic and adaptable approach, where continuous learning and anticipation of trends become part of daily operations.

Cultivating a Continuous Learning Mindset

To stay competitive, it is essential for the business and its employees to be constantly seeking new knowledge and skills. A mindset of continuous learning means embracing the idea that growth and improvement never end, and that everyone should commit to learning something new regularly.

Some practices to promote continuous learning include:

Encouraging Professional Development: Offer training, workshops, and access to online courses that allow employees to develop new skills and deepen their knowledge. This can be achieved through an education reimbursement policy or internal development programs.

Promoting Team Learning: Hold regular knowledge-sharing sessions where employees can present what they have learned at conferences, courses, or from books. This helps disseminate new knowledge throughout the organization.

Fostering Curiosity: Encourage employees to ask questions, explore new ideas, and stay updated on the latest trends and innovations in their fields.

When continuous learning is part of the organizational culture, the company becomes more resilient and capable of adapting quickly to changes.

Anticipating Market Trends

Anticipating market trends means being attentive to signs of change in the external environment and adjusting strategies before changes are fully established. This requires a proactive approach, which includes monitoring industry developments, analyzing consumer behavior, and keeping an eye on competitors' movements.

To effectively anticipate trends, consider the following practices:

Monitoring Trends and Innovations: Use market intelligence tools, attend events, and follow specialized publications to stay on top of the latest developments. This allows you to identify opportunities and threats before your competitors.

Analyzing Data and Consumer Behavior: Use data to understand customer needs and preferences. By analyzing buying patterns and feedback, you can predict changes in expectations and adjust the product or service offering.

Regular Benchmarking: Evaluate competitor performance and adopt best practices that can be applied to your business. This helps identify gaps and opportunities for improvement.

Anticipating trends enables the company to take proactive measures to adapt strategies, rather than reacting too late to market changes.

Constantly Adapting the Business Model

To stay competitive, it is essential to adapt the business model according to changing market conditions and new customer demands. This does not mean changing the company's identity, but rather adjusting approaches to remain relevant and meet ever-evolving expectations.

Some ways to adapt the business model include:

Diversifying Products and Services: Expand the portfolio of offerings to meet different market segments or emerging needs. Diversification can help reduce risks and explore new revenue streams.

Innovating Revenue Models: Consider new monetization methods, such as subscriptions, freemium models, or complementary services. This can generate additional revenue streams and increase customer loyalty.

Organizational Flexibility: Maintain an organizational structure that allows for rapid changes. This may include creating agile teams to develop new projects or adjusting operational processes to gain efficiency.

Constantly adapting the business model ensures that the company stays relevant and can seize new opportunities as they arise.

Practical Exercise: Preparing the Company for the Future

1. Develop a Continuous Learning Plan for the Team: Identify three areas of knowledge where the team could benefit from training and develop a plan to provide learning opportunities. Consider courses, workshops, or internal training sessions.

2. Monitor an Emerging Trend in Your Industry: Choose a trend or innovation gaining momentum in the sector and analyze its potential impact on your business. Propose actions that could be implemented to take advantage of the trend or mitigate risks.

3. Evaluate the Current Business Model and Propose Adjustments: Review the company's business model, considering opportunities for diversification or new revenue models. Identify a change that could improve competitiveness and develop an action plan to implement it.

m um mundo de constantes mudanças, manter um negócio relevante e competitivo exige proatividade e

Claudio Pinho Junior

Your Journey to a Self-Managing Business

Claudio Pinho Junior

Throughout this book, we have explored strategies and practices for transforming your business into a self-managed operation. The journey to achieve this goal requires dedication and a structured approach, but the benefits are undeniable: more freedom for the entrepreneur, greater operational efficiency, and a motivated team capable of functioning independently. In this conclusion, we will recap the key points covered, propose an action plan for implementing the changes, and reflect on the vision for the future of entrepreneurship.

Recap of Key Points

Architecting Your Self-Managed Business: We began by establishing the importance of defining a clear vision and identifying key processes for automation to reduce reliance on daily operations.

The Power of Efficient Processes: Consistency and standardization of processes are essential for business scalability. Mapping, eliminating bottlenecks, and documenting processes ensure smooth operations.

The Art of Effective Delegation: Delegating tasks allows leaders to focus on strategic activities. Creating a clear structure for delegation and overcoming the fear of losing control are fundamental steps.

Automating for Success: Automating manual tasks and implementing integrated systems help optimize resources and increase productivity.

Measuring Success: KPIs That Matter: Monitoring performance through KPIs is crucial for making informed decisions. The right indicators provide an objective view of progress and areas that need attention.

Leading from a Distance: With remote teams becoming a reality, adapting management practices to ensure communication, trust, and ongoing collaboration is more important than ever.

Cultivating Team Autonomy: Promoting a culture of responsibility and offering growth opportunities contribute to the development of autonomous teams.

Building a Championship Team: Recruiting and retaining top talent requires defining ideal profiles, implementing effective selection processes, and creating an attractive environment for employees.

Mastering Time for Leaders: Effective time management is essential for leaders to focus on what truly matters, using prioritization techniques, productive routines, and eliminating time-wasters.

Agility in Business: Quickly adapting to changes and implementing agile methodologies are key to staying competitive in a dynamic market.

Communication That Transforms: Establishing the right channels, implementing communication rituals, and promoting transparency are practices that ensure the flow of information and team alignment.

The Future is Now: Staying Ahead: Cultivating a mindset of continuous learning, anticipating trends, and constantly adapting the business model are essential actions for maintaining competitiveness in the long run.

Action Plan for Implementation

To effectively implement the ideas presented in this book, follow these steps:

Initial Assessment: Conduct a detailed analysis of the current state of your business, identifying strengths, areas for improvement, and critical processes that need immediate attention.

Set Priorities: Based on the assessment, define the areas to be addressed first. Prioritize actions that will have a significant and rapid impact on the operation.

Develop a Timeline: Create a plan with realistic deadlines for implementing the changes, involving the team and ensuring everyone is aware of the steps and goals to be achieved.

Empower Your Team: Provide training and resources for your team to adopt new practices with confidence. Cultural change is as important as operational changes.

Monitor and Adjust: Use KPIs to track progress and adjust the plan as needed. Continuous improvement should be a guiding principle, adapting strategies based on the results achieved.

Regular Reassessment: Every six months or annually, review the progress of the implementations and adjust priorities. Flexibility and adaptability are fundamental for a self-managed business.

Vision for the Future of Entrepreneurship

Entrepreneurship is constantly evolving, and the future promises even more accelerated changes driven by technology, new work models, and a globalized market. To thrive, entrepreneurs need to embrace a mindset of continuous learning, be open to innovation, and maintain the ability to adapt.

The concept of self-managed businesses will become increasingly important as the demand for flexibility and quality of life grows among professionals. Companies that embrace this philosophy, empowering their teams and creating agile and scalable processes, will be better positioned to face challenges and seize future opportunities.

The journey to transform a business into a self-managed operation is not simple, but it is a path that brings lasting rewards. Entrepreneurs who dedicate themselves to this journey are planting the seeds for long-term success, cultivating a resilient organization capable of growing and thriving regardless of the challenges that arise.

www.ingramcontent.com/pod-product-compliance
Lightning Source LLC
Chambersburg PA
CBHW050259230526
45471CB00005B/1955